Written & illustrated by Aleks Kashaev

THE ANXIOUS CREATURE

This book belongs to:

____

Disclaimer:

No part of this publication or the information in it may be quoted from or reproduced in any form by means such as printing, scanning, photocopying or otherwise without prior written permission of the copyright holder.

Terms of Use:

Effort has been made to ensure the information in this book is accurate and complete, however, the author and the publisher do not warrant the accuracy of the information, text and graphics contained within the book due to the rapid changing nature of science, research, known and unknown facts and internet.

The Author and the publisher do not hold any responsibility for errors, omission or contrary interpretation of the subject matter herein.

This book is presented solely for motivational and informational purposes only.

Hi! I'm Jitters, the Anxious Creature.

Sometimes when I think too much about something, I start to worry!

I have a recital later today.

What if I do bad?

It happens when I'm performing in front of others or competing in sports.

It happens when I'm about to meet someone new or try something I haven't before.

Sometimes, it makes me freeze. I feel like
I can't move or even speak!

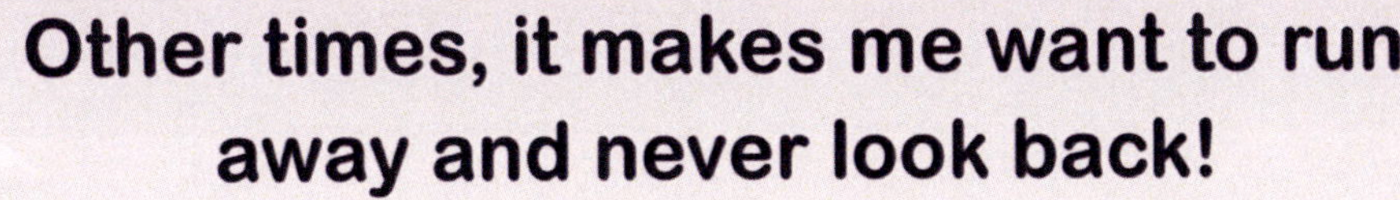

Other times, it makes me want to run away and never look back!

Anxiety can make me sad, angry and avoidant.

I feel my palms get sweaty and my legs get shaky.

The last time I felt anxious
was at my school recital.

I kept thinking about things that were out of my control.

What will everyone think?

What if I don't perform well?

What if something bad happens?

Luckily my friend Joy, the Positive Creature was performing at the recital with me.

She saw how anxious I was and came up to me.

She told me that feeling anxious is normal
and that everyone feels anxious at times.

When it happens, there are things we can do to help us calm down.

Joy then told me that we can use the

3-3-3
TECHNIQUE

to calm our minds and bodies
when we get anxious.

First, we find **3 things that we can see.** I looked around and saw a chair, a music sheet and a flute.

Then, we name 3 sounds that we could hear.
I heard talking, music playing and laughter.

Lastly, we move 3 parts of our bodies.
I moved my hands, legs and arms!

Focusing on what's around me took
my mind off my negative thoughts!

I thanked Joy for teaching me
how to to calm my anxiety.

Later that week, I had a soccer game that I was anxious about.

My negative thoughts returned!

What if we don't win?

What if I fail my team?

What if I get injured?

As the game was about to start, I saw my friend Joy in the crowd and remembered the 3-3-3 technique.

I found 3 things that I could see. I saw a soccer ball, a water bottle and a towl.

I listened to 3 things I could hear. I heard a bird chirping, a whistle blowing and leaves moving.

I moved 3 parts of my body. I moved my eyes, legs and fingers.

My anxiety began to shrink! We played our hardest that day and ended up winning!

From that day on, I always used the 3-3-3 technique when I felt anxiety coming on. I could now control it!

Dear Readers,

Thank you for your purchase!

I hope that you and your little one(s) enjoyed reading this book as much as I did making it. I made it with the goal of helping children manage anxiety in tough moments.

I'm motivated to continue making impactful children's books to help kids grow. Without you, my mission would not be possible!

I've included a QR code that will send you and your little one(s) free coloring pages.

I would greatly appreciate it if you could leave a review for my book. This will help immensely to get it into the hands of more readers. Any feedback will also be very helpful in making future books the best they could possibly be!

Find your way to the end of this maze by following 

WORD FIND PUZZLE

C	F	A	V	T	H	R	E	E
H	V	W	O	R	R	Y	J	C
O	M	O	A	B	I	O	A	A
I	S	D	I	Y	Y	E	L	L
C	B	U	E	D	T	H	T	M
J	I	T	T	E	R	S	J	S

Find these hidden words:

WORRY CALM JITTERS THREE JOY

Copy each picture into the empty grid.

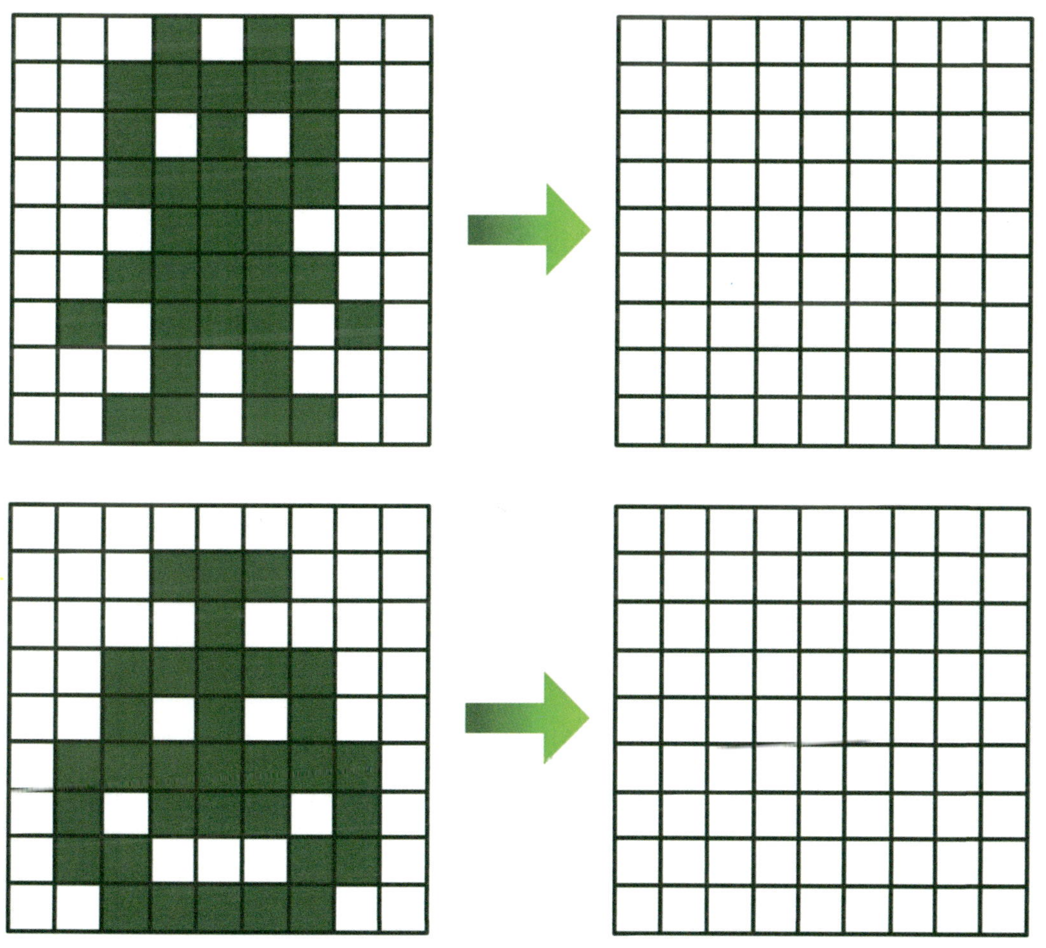

Made in the USA
Las Vegas, NV
04 May 2024

89536794R00021